CW01431702

MICHAEL SOUTHERN SR.

The Mighty Samson: The Legend of Israel's Champion

WHIMSICAL WONDERS

First published by Self-Published 2024

Copyright © 2024 by Michael Southern Sr.

First edition

This book was professionally typeset on Reedsy.
Find out more at reedsy.com

To Tyler,

This book is dedicated to you, a young boy whose strength and determination inspire everyone around you. Like Samson, you have a heart full of courage and perseverance. As you grow, always remember that true strength comes not only from within, but from trusting in God. Keep believing in yourself and in His plan for your life, and never give up on the amazing things you are destined to achieve. You are a true champion in every way—stay strong and keep your faith

.

"Strength does not come from our own power, but from our faith in the One True God. In every battle we face, it is not by might nor by power, but by the Spirit of the Lord that we find victory. Like Samson, we may fall, we may face great trials, but through faith, we rise again. Let us remember that true strength is born from trusting in God, for in Him, all things are possible."

– Inspired by the story of Samson

Contents

Foreword

The story of Samson is one of the most captivating and powerful tales in the Bible. It's a story that speaks to the heart of what true strength means—not just physical power, but the inner strength that comes from faith in God. Samson's life was filled with great victories and painful struggles, much like the challenges we all face. But through it all, the lesson remains clear: real power comes not from our own hands, but from trusting in the One True God.

This book was written with the hope of inspiring young readers to see that strength isn't just about muscles or might—it's about having the courage to stand for what is right, the perseverance to keep going even when things are hard, and the faith to believe that God has a plan for each of us. Samson's journey shows us that even when we fall, God is always there to lift us up and give us the strength we need to fulfill our purpose.

As you read about Samson's incredible feats, his challenges, and his ultimate sacrifice, may you be reminded that you, too, have the strength within you to overcome whatever life may bring—especially when you trust in God.

Preface

The story of Samson has always captivated the imaginations of readers for generations. It's a tale of great strength, courage, and the incredible power that comes from God. But Samson's story is more than just about a man with extraordinary strength—it's a story about faith, redemption, and the consequences of the choices we make.

In writing The Mighty Samson: The Legend of Israel's Champion, my hope is to bring this timeless story to life for young readers. Samson's journey from a chosen child with unmatched strength to a man who faces betrayal, loss, and ultimate redemption, is filled with lessons for all ages. It teaches us that even the strongest among us can fall, but with faith in God, we can rise again.

This book is designed to be engaging, accessible, and inspiring for children, presenting Samson's adventures in a way that is both exciting and faithful to the original story from the Bible. I've aimed to keep the core message of trusting in God at the forefront, while showing that real strength comes from within—when we align ourselves with God's purpose.

I hope this book will inspire and encourage its readers, reminding them that no matter the challenges they face, faith in God will always guide them to victory.

Acknowledgments

First and foremost, I want to thank God for His endless grace and guidance throughout this journey. It is through His strength and wisdom that I have been able to bring this story to life. Every word written is a reflection of His purpose and a reminder of the power that comes from trusting in Him.

To my amazing wife, your unwavering support and love have been my greatest blessing. You have been my constant source of encouragement, and without you, this book would not have been possible. Thank you for believing in me, for standing by me in every moment, and for always being my biggest champion. You have always been there for our family when we needed you the most. You work tirelessly day in and day out when we couldn't just to make sure we have what we need. You truly are the greatest champion of them all.

To my children, who inspire me every day with their curiosity and joy, this book is as much for you as it is for all the young readers who will enjoy it. Your love has given me the strength to persevere, and I hope this story will encourage you to always trust in God's plan for your lives. Even though you are all grown, you still inspire me to want to do better. I just hope I am still a champion in your eyes. As long as we put God first, all things are possible.

To my dearest friends, we most continue to inspire each other to be great to to continue to look unto God first. My closest friends (you know who you are) you continue to walk by my side and pick me up when I fall. You inspire me to always want to keep going. Much love and respect.

Finally, to all the readers and supporters, thank you for your interest in this book. My hope is that it brings joy, inspiration, and a reminder that no matter what we face, we can always find strength in God.

Prologue

Long ago, in the land of Israel, the people faced a time of great hardship. They had turned away from the One True God and fell under the harsh rule of their enemies, the Philistines. The Philistines were cruel, and the Israelites, desperate for deliverance, cried out for help. It was in this time of darkness that God had a plan—a plan to raise up a champion who would lead His people to freedom.

This champion's name was Samson. Even before he was born, Samson was chosen by God for a special purpose. His life was to be one of incredible strength, but not just in his body—his true strength would come from his faith in God. Samson's journey was not an easy one. Along the way, he would face betrayal, temptation, and challenges that would test his very soul.

But in the end, Samson's story reminds us of the power of faith, the consequences of our choices, and the redemption that is always possible through God. This is the story of Samson—a story of strength, courage, and the unwavering power of God's plan.

Introduction

A long time ago, in a land called Israel, there lived a special boy named Samson. His story began before he was even born, when the people of Israel were facing great trouble. They had turned away from the One True God and had fallen under the rule of their enemies, the Philistines. The Philistines were strong and cruel, and the Israelites cried out for help.

One day, an angel appeared to a woman who had no children. The angel told her that she would have a son, and he would grow up to save the people of Israel. But there was something important about this boy—he would be different from other children. God had a special plan for him. The angel said Samson would have great strength, as long as he followed God's rules, and never cut his hair.

From the moment Samson was born, his parents knew he was destined for something great. He would become a hero, a mighty champion chosen by God to defeat Israel's enemies. But Samson's journey would not be easy. His story is one of strength, faith, and the challenges that come with having such great power. This is the legend of Samson.

1

A Promise from Heaven

Many years ago, the people of Israel were in great trouble. They had forgotten the ways of the One True God and had fallen into the hands of the Philistines, a powerful group of people who ruled over them. The Israelites were sad and afraid because the Philistines were harsh rulers. They needed a hero, someone who could save them from their enemies. Little did they know, God had a special plan to send them a mighty champion.

In a small town of Israel, there lived a man named Manoah and his wife. Manoah and his wife had no children, and this made them very sad. But one day, something extraordinary happened. An angel of the Lord appeared to Manoah's wife. The angel was shining brightly and spoke with a voice that was both gentle and powerful. The angel told her, "You will have a son. He will be a special child, chosen by God to help deliver Israel from the Philistines. But there is something you must do. You must never cut his hair, for he will be a Nazirite, dedicated to God from birth."

Manoah's wife was amazed by what the angel had told her. She quickly ran to tell her husband the wonderful news. "A man of God came to me!" she said. "He told me that we will have a son who will be strong and mighty. He will be the one to save our people!"

Manoah, filled with wonder and joy, prayed to God. He asked God to send the angel again so that they could know more about how to raise this special child. God heard Manoah's prayer, and once again, the angel appeared. This time, both Manoah and his wife were there to listen carefully to the angel's message. The angel repeated the instructions: "Your son must never drink wine, and you must never cut his hair, for he will be a Nazirite, chosen by God to deliver Israel."

When the angel had finished speaking, he rose up into the sky and disappeared. Manoah and his wife knew that this was a message from God, and they praised Him for His great plan. They could hardly wait for the day their son would be born.

Months passed, and finally, the day came. Manoah's wife gave birth to a healthy baby boy. They named him Samson, just as the angel had said. From the very beginning, Samson was different. His parents could see that God was with him. They watched over him carefully, making sure that they followed all of the instructions the angel had given them.

As Samson grew, it became clear that he was not like other boys. He was incredibly strong, even as a child. He could lift heavy objects with ease, and his strength only grew as he got older. But it wasn't just his physical strength that made Samson special. God's Spirit was with him, guiding him and preparing him for the great things he would do.

One day, when Samson was still a young man, he felt something stir inside him. It was as if God was calling him to begin his mission. Samson knew that his time had come to face the enemies of Israel, the Philistines. He was ready to take on the challenge, for he had been born for this very purpose.

But Samson's journey would not be an easy one. He would face many trials and make mistakes along the way. Even though he had been chosen by God, Samson would have to learn that true strength comes not just from muscles but from trusting in the One True God.

As Samson set out on his path, his parents watched with pride and hope. They knew that their son was destined for greatness, but they also knew that he would need to stay close to God to succeed in his mission. Samson's story was only just beginning, and the challenges ahead would test him in ways he could never have imagined.

The legend of Samson, the mighty champion of Israel, was about to unfold.

He would become a hero, feared by his enemies and loved by his people. But Samson would also learn that with great power comes great responsibility, and that even the strongest man can only be strong when he follows the will of God.

And so, Samson took his first steps toward his destiny, ready to face whatever lay ahead. Little did he know, his greatest battles were yet to come. But with God's help, Samson would rise to become one of the greatest heroes Israel had ever known.

2

The Secret of Samson's Strength

As Samson grew older, his strength became legendary throughout the land of Israel. Everyone marveled at how powerful he was. No one could understand how he could lift the heaviest stones, break thick ropes as if they were threads, or run faster than any man. The secret of his strength, however, was not something anyone could see—it came from his special vow to God.

Samson's parents had faithfully followed the instructions given to them by the angel. They never cut Samson's hair, and as long as his hair remained uncut, his strength was unmatched. But Samson's incredible power wasn't just for show. God had a purpose for him—to defeat the enemies of Israel, the Philistines.

One day, Samson decided to visit a town called Timnath, which was near the land of the Philistines. As he walked along the road, something surprising happened. Suddenly, a young lion sprang out from the bushes, roaring and charging toward Samson! Most people would have run away in fear, but Samson didn't flinch. God's Spirit came upon him, and Samson grabbed the lion with his bare hands. With one powerful move, he tore the lion apart as if it were a small animal.

After defeating the lion, Samson continued on his journey. He didn't tell anyone what had happened, not even his parents. But Samson knew that his strength was not his own—it was a gift from the One True God. And this was just the beginning of the mighty acts he would perform.

As time went on, Samson began to feel drawn to the Philistines, not just to defeat them, but because of a woman he had seen in Timnath. This woman was a Philistine, and though Samson's parents tried to warn him, saying, "Is there no woman among the daughters of your people that you must go to the Philistines?" Samson was determined to marry her. He believed this was part of God's plan, even though it puzzled his parents.

Samson's wedding plans soon set the stage for one of his greatest feats of strength. During the wedding feast, Samson challenged the Philistines with a riddle. "Out of the eater came forth meat, and out of the strong came forth sweetness," he said, referring to the lion he had killed earlier. He promised that if they could solve the riddle within seven days, he would give them thirty sets of clothes. But if they couldn't solve it, they would have to give him the thirty sets of clothes instead.

The Philistines tried everything to solve the riddle, but no one could figure it out. Frustrated, they went to Samson's bride and pressured her to find the answer. She begged and cried until Samson finally told her the secret. She quickly revealed the answer to the Philistines, and they came back to Samson with the solution.

Samson was furious when he realized they had cheated. Filled with anger, he went down to a nearby town, struck down thirty Philistines, and took their clothes to pay his debt. This act of strength left the Philistines angry and afraid, and Samson knew that his battle with them had only just begun.

From that moment, the Philistines began to see Samson as a dangerous enemy. They were determined to find a way to defeat him, but Samson's strength, as long as his hair remained uncut, seemed unstoppable. Time after time, Samson would rise up against them, using his strength to defend the people of Israel.

One day, Samson's enemies plotted to capture him. They waited for him in the city of Gaza, hoping to trap him while he was asleep. But Samson, with God's strength, broke free from their trap, lifting the massive gates of the city off their hinges and carrying them up a hill! No matter what the Philistines tried, they could not defeat Samson.

As Samson's victories grew, so did his confidence. But there was one thing that would always remain his greatest challenge: the secret of his strength. Only Samson and his parents knew that his strength came from his hair and his vow to God. Yet, Samson began to believe that his strength was his own, and this would lead him down a dangerous path.

While Samson was a mighty warrior, he often made mistakes. He didn't always listen to wise advice, and his heart sometimes led him into trouble. But through it all, God was with him, guiding him and giving him strength for the battles ahead.

The Philistines, however, were not done with Samson. They knew they could not defeat him with weapons or strength, so they plotted to find out the secret of his power. They would soon use trickery and deceit to try and uncover the one thing that could bring Samson down.

Samson's journey was far from over. His incredible feats of strength had made him a hero to the people of Israel, but his greatest challenges were still ahead. Would he remain faithful to God, or would his enemies discover the secret that could take away his strength? Only time would tell.

3

The Roaring Lion: Samson's First Battle

Samson was growing stronger by the day, and with each passing year, the stories of his strength spread throughout Israel and even into the land of the Philistines. everyone whispered about the young man who had torn apart a lion with his bare hands. But that lion was only the beginning of Samson's battles. As he grew older, his destiny as Israel's champion was just starting to unfold.

One day, while walking through the vineyards near Timnath, Samson came across something that caught his eye. It was the same place where he had fought the lion long ago. He approached the spot, remembering how God had given him the strength to defeat the wild beast. But when he reached the lion's carcass, Samson was surprised by what he saw.

Inside the lion's body, bees had made a hive, and it was filled with sweet honey! Samson reached inside and scooped out some of the honey, tasting its sweetness. He smiled to himself, for this honey seemed like a gift from God, a reminder of his strength and victories. He even took some of the honey back to his parents, but he didn't tell them where it had come from.

Though Samson had defeated the lion, his greatest battles were still ahead. The Philistines, Israel's enemies, continued to oppress the people. They were cruel and unkind, and the Israelites lived in fear. Samson knew that he was meant to change that. God had given him his great strength for a reason, and soon, he would have to use it in even bigger ways.

After his wedding in Timnath, things became tense between Samson and the Philistines. They had tricked him into revealing the answer to his riddle, and in return, he had struck down thirty of their men to settle the score. The Philistines were furious with Samson, and they wanted revenge. They plotted to take down this mighty warrior who had humiliated them.

One day, the Philistines learned that Samson was staying in a town called Lehi. They gathered a large group of soldiers and surrounded the town, determined to capture him once and for all. The men of Judah, Samson's own people, were terrified. They knew that if they didn't do something, the Philistines would destroy their town.

The leaders of Judah came to Samson with trembling hearts. "Samson," they said, "the Philistines have come to take you. They are angry, and if we don't hand you over to them, they will destroy us. Please, let us bind you and give you to them. We won't hurt you, but we need to save ourselves."

Samson looked at the men of Judah with understanding. He knew they were afraid, but he also knew that God was with him. "Very well," Samson said, "but promise me that you will not harm me yourselves."

The men of Judah agreed and bound Samson with new ropes. They led him out of the town, where the Philistines were waiting. As the Philistines saw Samson being led toward them, they began to shout in victory. They thought they had finally captured the mighty Samson, the one who had caused them so much trouble.

But just as they approached him, something incredible happened. The Spirit of the Lord came upon Samson with great power, and in an instant, he snapped the ropes that bound him as if they were thin pieces of thread. The Philistines stopped in their tracks, shocked by what they had just seen. Samson was free, and he was stronger than ever.

Looking around, Samson spotted the jawbone of a donkey lying on the ground. He picked it up, and with this simple weapon, he charged at the Philistines. In a mighty display of strength, Samson struck down one Philistine after another. By the time the battle was over, Samson had defeated a thousand men with nothing more than the jawbone in his hand!

When the battle was finished, Samson stood tall, victorious over his enemies.

He knew that it wasn't just his own strength that had won the day—it was the strength that came from the One True God. Samson lifted the jawbone and called out, "With the jawbone of a donkey, heaps upon heaps, I have slain a thousand men!"

But after the battle, Samson grew very thirsty. He had used so much of his strength that he felt weak and exhausted. He cried out to God, saying, "O Lord, You have given me this great victory, but now I am dying of thirst! Will You let me fall into the hands of my enemies?"

God heard Samson's prayer and answered him in a miraculous way. Suddenly, water began to flow from a rock near where Samson stood. He drank from it, and his strength was restored. Samson knew that God had not abandoned him. No matter how strong he was, he still needed God's help in every battle.

From that day on, the place where Samson had defeated the Philistines was called Ramath-Lehi, which means "Jawbone Hill." The story of Samson's great victory spread far and wide, and the Philistines grew even more fearful of him. They knew that no matter how hard they tried, they could not defeat this man who fought with the power of God.

But while Samson's strength had brought victory, his journey was far from over. More challenges lay ahead, and his greatest test was still to come. For there were those who wanted to discover the secret of his strength, and they would stop at nothing to bring down Israel's mighty champion.

4

Samson's Riddle: A Trick to Fool His Enemies

As Samson continued to grow in strength and fame, his story reached every corner of Israel and beyond. The people of Israel looked to him as their protector, and the Philistines feared him as their greatest enemy. Yet, despite all his victories, Samson still had a weakness that would lead him into danger: his heart. This weakness would soon bring him face to face with one of his greatest challenges.

Samson's heart led him to a Philistine woman from the town of Timnath. Despite the warnings of his parents and the knowledge that the Philistines were Israel's enemies, Samson insisted on marrying her. His parents were worried. "Is there no woman among the daughters of Israel that you must go to the Philistines?" they asked.

But Samson believed this was part of God's plan, though he did not know exactly how. He convinced his parents to arrange the marriage, and soon a great feast was prepared in Timnath to celebrate. This feast was filled with the Philistine lords and leaders, men who would soon discover that Samson was not only strong but also very clever.

During the feast, Samson decided to test the Philistines with a riddle. He stood before them with a mischievous grin and said, "I will give you a riddle. If you can solve it within the seven days of the feast, I will give you thirty sets of clothes. But if you cannot solve it, you must give me thirty sets of clothes."

The Philistines, thinking this was a simple game, agreed. They listened closely as Samson spoke the riddle: "Out of the eater came forth meat, and out of the strong came forth sweetness."

The Philistines were puzzled. They whispered among themselves, trying to figure out the answer. But no matter how hard they thought, they could not solve the riddle. Each day, they became more and more frustrated. They didn't want to lose the bet, but the answer seemed impossible to find.

As the days of the feast passed, the Philistines grew desperate. Finally, on the fourth day, they went to Samson's new wife and demanded her help. "Entice your husband to tell us the answer to his riddle," they said, "or we will burn you and your father's house with fire. Did you invite us here to make us poor?"

Samson's wife was terrified. She didn't want to betray her husband, but she feared the Philistines even more. So she went to Samson and began to weep. "You don't love me," she cried, "because you haven't told me the answer to your riddle!"

At first, Samson resisted. "I haven't even told my parents," he said. "Why should I tell you?" But his wife continued to plead and cry throughout the rest of the feast. Finally, on the seventh day, Samson could stand it no longer. He told her the answer, trusting her to keep it secret.

But instead of keeping his trust, Samson's wife quickly ran to the Philistines and told them the answer. Armed with this new information, the Philistines returned to Samson with smug smiles on their faces. "What is sweeter than honey?" they said. "And what is stronger than a lion?"

Samson's face darkened as he realized what had happened. They had cheated, using his own wife to betray him. Filled with anger, he replied, "If you had not plowed with my heifer, you would not have solved my riddle."

Though Samson was furious, he was bound by his word. He owed the Philistines thirty sets of clothes. But instead of simply buying them, Samson did something no one expected. He went to the nearby town of Ashkelon, where he struck down thirty Philistines, taking their clothes and giving them to the men who had answered the riddle.

After this, Samson returned to his father's house, leaving his wife behind in Timnath. His heart was heavy with anger and betrayal. He had trusted his wife, and she had betrayed him. But Samson's anger toward the Philistines only grew stronger. He knew that his battle with them was far from over.

Meanwhile, the Philistines thought they had won a small victory over Samson. But little did they know, their deceitful actions would only provoke him to strike back harder. Samson's strength was not just in his muscles—it was in his spirit, and when he felt wronged, his anger could become as powerful as his fists.

In time, Samson returned to Timnath, wanting to visit his wife. But when he arrived, he was met with even more betrayal. Her father had given her to another man, thinking that Samson had abandoned her for good. Samson's heart burned with fury.

Feeling wronged once again, Samson decided to take revenge on the Philistines in a most unusual way. He caught 300 foxes and tied their tails together in pairs, attaching a burning torch to each pair. Then he set the foxes loose in the Philistines' grain fields, vineyards, and olive groves. The fire spread quickly, destroying their crops and causing great damage to their land.

The Philistines were outraged when they discovered what Samson had done. They demanded to know who was responsible, and when they learned it was Samson, they took revenge on his wife and her father, burning them to death.

This cycle of betrayal and revenge deepened the conflict between Samson and the Philistines. His great strength and cleverness had made him their worst enemy. But Samson's story was far from over, and the battles between him and the Philistines were only just beginning.

Samson's strength came from God, and though he was often led by his emotions, God had a plan for him that was not yet complete. The Philistines would continue to seek ways to bring down Israel's champion, but as long as Samson trusted in the One True God, his strength would remain unmatched.

5

A Thousand Enemies: Samson's Greatest Victory

S amson had faced many trials and challenges, but none were as fierce as the Philistines. Their anger toward him grew after he had burned their fields and vineyards. They had tried to defeat him before, but each time they underestimated the power that God had given him. Now, the Philistines were more determined than ever to capture Samson and bring an end to his strength.

After the events in Timnath, Samson had gone into hiding. He retreated to a cave in the land of Etam, but the Philistines did not forget him. They marched into Judah with a massive army, demanding that the israelites hand over Samson or face destruction. The men of Judah, terrified of the Philistines, knew they had no choice but to find Samson and deliver him to their enemies.

Three thousand men from Judah went to the cave where Samson was hiding. They were afraid of both Samson's strength and the wrath of the Philistines. When they found Samson, they pleaded with him, saying, "Do you not know that the Philistines rule over us? Why have you done this to us? They will destroy us because of you!"

Samson looked at his fellow Israelites and understood their fear. He knew they were caught between his actions and the anger of the Philistines. "Promise me this," Samson said, "that you will not kill me yourselves. Bind me and deliver me to the Philistines, but do not harm me."

The men of Judah agreed. They tied Samson with strong, new ropes and led him to the Philistines, who were waiting with a great army. As soon as the Philistines saw Samson being led toward them, they began to shout in victory. They thought they had finally captured the man who had caused them so much trouble.

But just as the Philistines closed in, something incredible happened. The Spirit of the Lord came upon Samson with great power. In an instant, he snapped the ropes that bound him as if they were thin threads. The Philistines stopped in their tracks, fear spreading across their faces as they realized that Samson was free, and his strength had returned.

Samson looked around for a weapon, but there was nothing at hand—nothing except the jawbone of a donkey lying on the ground. Without hesitation, Samson picked up the jawbone and charged into the Philistine army. With nothing more than this simple weapon, he began to strike down his enemies.

The Philistines were no match for Samson's strength. One by one, they fell before him as he swung the jawbone with mighty force. The sounds of the battle echoed across the land as Samson fought with the power of God, defeating hundreds of Philistines. The soldiers who remained tried to flee, but Samson's strength was unstoppable. By the time the battle was over, Samson had struck down a thousand Philistines with the jawbone of a donkey.

When the dust had settled, Samson stood alone on the battlefield, surrounded by the fallen bodies of his enemies. He raised the jawbone high and called out, "With the jawbone of a donkey, heaps upon heaps, I have slain a thousand men!" It was a victory unlike any other, and it showed the Philistines just how powerful Samson truly was when he fought with the strength of the One True God.

But after the battle, Samson was exhausted. His body ached, and he was overcome with thirst. He felt as though he would die if he didn't have water soon. In desperation, he cried out to God, saying, "O Lord, You have given me this great victory. But now, must I die of thirst and fall into the hands of the uncircumcised?"

God heard Samson's cry and answered him in a miraculous way. Suddenly, a spring of water burst forth from the ground, right where Samson stood. He drank from it, and his strength returned. Refreshed and renewed, Samson knew that God had provided for him once again. The place where the water flowed was called En-hakkore, which means "the spring of him who called," and it became a symbol of how God had answered Samson's prayer in his time of need.

After this victory, Samson continued to judge Israel for twenty years. During that time, the Philistines did not dare to challenge him again. They knew that Samson's strength was beyond anything they could defeat, for it came from God Himself.

However, even though Samson had defeated many enemies, he still faced battles within his own heart. He struggled with pride, and sometimes he forgot that his strength was a gift from God, not something he had earned on his own. This pride would eventually lead Samson into dangerous situations, but for now, he was Israel's champion, and the people looked to him for protection and guidance.

As the years passed, Samson's legend grew, and his victories over the Philistines became the stories that parents told their children. But the Philistines had not forgotten their hatred for Samson. They continued to search for a way to bring him down, waiting for the moment when they could finally defeat Israel's mighty warrior.

Little did Samson know, that moment was fast approaching. His greatest battle was yet to come, and it would not be fought with strength alone. Samson would soon face an enemy who sought to destroy him, not with swords or spears, but with deception and betrayal.

The story of Samson was far from over. His journey had been filled with great victories, but the challenges ahead would test not only his strength but also his heart. Would Samson remain faithful to the One True God, or would his enemies find a way to take away his strength forever? Only time would tell.

6

Samson and Delilah: The Secret Revealed

As Samson continued to lead Israel, his fame and strength only grew. The people of Israel looked to him for protection, and the Philistines dreaded the thought of facing him in battle. But Samson's greatest weakness had never been his enemies; it was his own heart. And soon, this weakness would lead him into a trap unlike any he had faced before.

In the land of the Philistines, there was a woman named Delilah. She was known for her beauty and her charm, and it wasn't long before Samson fell in love with her. Even though Delilah was a Philistine, Samson's heart was drawn to her. He visited her often, spending much of his time with her. But what Samson didn't know was that the Philistine leaders had their own plans for Delilah.

The Philistines knew that they could not defeat Samson with weapons, but perhaps they could defeat him through deception. They went to Delilah with an offer she could not refuse. "Entice Samson to tell you the secret of his strength," they said, "and we will each give you eleven hundred pieces of silver." Delilah agreed, and from that moment on, she began to work on discovering the secret of Samson's mighty power.

One evening, as Samson sat with Delilah, she asked him, "Tell me, I pray thee, wherein thy great strength lieth, and wherewith thou mightest be bound to afflict thee?" She spoke sweetly, as if it were just a game, but Samson could sense something behind her words. Instead of telling her the truth, he decided to tease her with a false answer.

"If they bind me with seven fresh bowstrings that have not been dried," Samson said, "then I shall be as weak as any other man."

Delilah listened carefully and waited for her chance. Later, while Samson slept, she secretly bound him with seven fresh bowstrings. Then she called out, "The Philistines are upon thee, Samson!" Samson awoke and easily snapped the bowstrings, his strength still intact. Delilah had failed, but she was not ready to give up.

The next time Delilah asked him about his strength, Samson gave her another false answer. "If they bind me with new ropes that have never been used," he said, "then I shall become weak and be like any other man."

Again, Delilah waited for her moment. She bound Samson with new ropes while he slept and called out, "The Philistines are upon thee, Samson!" But once again, Samson snapped the ropes with ease. His strength remained, and Delilah's plan was foiled again.

But Delilah was determined. She pressed Samson day after day, pleading with him to reveal the truth. She cried and begged, accusing him of not loving her because he kept lying to her. Samson, weary from her constant questioning, finally told her yet another false story. "If you weave the seven locks of my head with a loom and fasten it," he said, "then I shall be weak."

Delilah tried it, weaving Samson's hair into the loom while he slept. She called out once more, "The Philistines are upon thee, Samson!" But Samson awoke, pulled the loom from his hair, and stood strong as ever. Delilah was furious, and she knew she had to find the real answer.

Finally, after days of constant pleading, Samson could resist no longer. His heart was worn down, and he made a decision he would soon regret. He revealed the truth to Delilah. "No razor has ever come upon my head," he said, "for I have been a Nazirite to God from my mother's womb. If my hair is cut, then my strength will leave me, and I will become weak like any other man."

Delilah knew that this time Samson had told her the truth. She quickly sent word to the Philistine leaders, telling them to come at once. That night, as Samson slept, Delilah took a razor and cut off the seven locks of his hair.

The power that had made Samson strong was gone.

When Samson awoke, Delilah called out as she had before, "The Philistines are upon thee, Samson!" But this time, things were different. Samson rose to fight, just as he had before, but his strength was gone. He tried to break free, but he was no stronger than an ordinary man. The Philistines seized him, capturing him at last.

The Philistines were overjoyed. They had finally captured the mighty Samson. But they were not satisfied with simply defeating him. They wanted to make an example of him. They took Samson to Gaza, where they bound him in chains and blinded him by putting out his eyes. Samson, once the strongest man in Israel, was now a prisoner, helpless and broken.

The Philistines forced Samson to work as a slave, grinding grain in their prison. They laughed and mocked him, thinking that they had finally won. But what they didn't realize was that Samson's story was not over. For even though Samson had lost his strength, God had not forgotten him.

As Samson worked in the prison, something began to happen. His hair, the source of his strength, began to grow back. Though his body was weak, his faith in God was being restored. Samson realized that his true strength had always come from the One True God, not just from his hair.

The Philistines, however, were still celebrating their victory. They decided to hold a great feast in honor of their god, Dagon, and they brought Samson out to mock him before the crowd. They placed him in the middle of a large temple, where thousands of Philistines gathered to celebrate. But Samson had one last request—one final prayer to the God who had given him his strength.

7

The Mighty Fall: Samson's Strength Is Lost

S amson, once the mighty champion of Israel, now found himself weak, blind, and chained in a Philistine prison. The once great warrior who had struck down a thousand men with a donkey's jawbone was now reduced to grinding grain like a common slave. His head, once crowned with the long hair that was the symbol of his strength, was now shaven, and the power he had from the One True God seemed to have left him.

But even in this lowly state, Samson had not been forgotten by God. Though his strength was gone, and his eyes were blinded, Samson's faith began to grow again. In the darkness of the prison, Samson had time to think, to reflect on the mistakes he had made. He realized that his strength had never truly been his own—it had always been a gift from God. Samson began to pray again, seeking God's forgiveness and help.

Meanwhile, the Philistines were rejoicing. They believed they had finally defeated their greatest enemy, the man who had caused them so much trouble. They praised their false god, Dagon, believing that he had delivered Samson into their hands. But what the Philistines didn't know was that Samson's hair had begun to grow back. Slowly but surely, the symbol of his Nazirite vow returned, and with it, the promise of God's power.

The Philistine leaders decided to hold a great feast in the temple of Dagon to celebrate their victory over Samson. Thousands of people gathered for the event, filling the temple with laughter, music, and praise for their god. In their pride, they wanted to make a spectacle of Samson. They ordered that he be brought from the prison so that they could mock him in front of the crowd.

Samson was led into the temple by a young servant, his hands bound, his steps unsure because of his blindness. The Philistines jeered at him, shouting insults and laughing at the once-mighty warrior. They thought that Samson was completely defeated, but they did not realize that God still had a plan for him.

As Samson stood in the temple, he listened to the voices of the Philistines celebrating their false god. His heart was heavy with the weight of his mistakes, but he knew that God was still with him. Samson asked the servant who led him, "Let me feel the pillars upon which the temple stands, that I may lean upon them." The servant, thinking nothing of it, guided Samson to the two central pillars that held up the temple.

As Samson stood between the pillars, he raised his face to the heavens, though he could not see. He prayed to God with all his heart, saying, "O Lord God, remember me, I pray thee. Strengthen me, I pray thee, only this once, O God, that I may be avenged of the Philistines for my two eyes."

With his hands resting on the pillars, Samson could feel the strength returning to his body. The power of God surged through him once more, just as it had in the past. Samson knew that this would be his final act, but he was willing to give his life to defeat the enemies of Israel and to show the Philistines that the One True God was mightier than any false idol.

With all his might, Samson pushed against the pillars. At first, the crowd did not notice, still too busy celebrating and mocking him. But as the pillars began to shift and crack, a sudden hush fell over the temple. The ground trembled as the great stone columns started to give way under Samson's incredible strength.

Samson cried out with a mighty voice, "Let me die with the Philistines!" With one final, powerful push, the pillars collapsed, and the entire temple began to crumble. The roof caved in, and the walls came tumbling down, crushing the Philistine lords and all the people inside. The great temple of Dagon was destroyed in an instant.

In that moment, Samson gave his life, but in doing so, he defeated more Philistines than he had in all his previous battles combined. The Philistines who had mocked him were now gone, and their victory celebration turned to dust.

As the temple lay in ruins, Samson's family came to retrieve his body. They brought him back to his homeland and buried him in the tomb of his father, Manoah. Samson's story came to an end, but his legacy lived on. For twenty years, he had judged Israel and fought against the enemies of God's people. His strength and courage, though sometimes misused, had been part of God's plan to deliver Israel from the Philistines.

Samson's life was a lesson in both the power of God and the dangers of pride. He had been chosen from birth to be a mighty warrior, and though he had made many mistakes, God never abandoned him. In the end, Samson's faith was restored, and he fulfilled his purpose as Israel's champion.

The people of Israel remembered Samson not just for his incredible strength, but for his final act of sacrifice. He had given everything, even his life, to defeat the enemies of God's people. And through his story, they were reminded that true strength comes not from muscles or weapons, but from trusting in the One True God.

Though Samson's life was filled with challenges, his story is one of redemption and faith. He was not perfect, but God used him in mighty ways. And in the end, Samson's greatest victory came not from the battles he fought, but from the moment he trusted God fully, even in his weakest hour.

8

A Prisoner in Chains: Samson's Darkest Days

Samson's fall from glory was swift and painful. Once the mighty champion of Israel, he was now a blind and broken man, bound in chains and held captive by the Philistines. The same enemies he had once defeated now laughed at him as they paraded him through the streets. Samson, who had once struck fear into the hearts of his foes, was now a prisoner in the Philistine city of Gaza, the place where he had once carried away the city gates with his bare hands.

The Philistines didn't just imprison Samson—they wanted to make him suffer. They blinded him, taking away his sight, and forced him to do the work of an animal. Day after day, Samson pushed the heavy grinding stone, turning grain into flour for his captors. It was humiliating work, and the Philistines took pleasure in seeing their greatest enemy brought so low. They believed that their god, Dagon, had finally delivered Samson into their hands, and they celebrated their victory with feasts and sacrifices.

But even in this dark time, Samson's faith was being renewed. While he worked in the prison, Samson had time to think and reflect on his life. He remembered the victories God had given him, and he also remembered the mistakes he had made. Samson realized that he had not always used his strength for the right reasons. He had often acted out of anger, pride, and selfishness, forgetting that his strength was a gift from the One True God.

As the days turned into weeks, something began to change. Slowly, Samson's hair started to grow back. It was a sign that God had not abandoned him, even in his darkest hour. Samson began to pray again, asking God to remember him and restore his strength. Though he was still a prisoner, Samson's heart was turning back to God, and his faith was being strengthened in the midst of his suffering.

The Philistines, however, continued to celebrate their triumph over Samson. They believed that his strength was gone forever and that there was nothing he could do to harm them anymore. They planned a great feast to honor their god, Dagon, for delivering Samson into their hands. The leaders of the Philistines gathered in a huge temple, where thousands of people filled the building to join in the celebration.

As part of their festivities, the Philistines decided to bring Samson out of the prison and put him on display. They wanted to mock him, to show everyone how the mighty warrior had been defeated. They believed that Samson was powerless, and they wanted to humiliate him in front of the crowd.

Samson was led out of the prison by a young servant. His once strong and confident steps were now slow and uncertain, as he could no longer see. The crowd roared with laughter as Samson was brought before them, but Samson didn't listen to their taunts. He knew that this might be his last chance to fulfill the purpose God had given him.

As the servant led him through the temple, Samson asked quietly, "Let me feel the pillars that support the temple, so I can lean against them." The servant, thinking it was a simple request, guided Samson to the two central pillars that held up the temple. Samson placed his hands on the pillars, and though he couldn't see, he knew exactly where he was.

In that moment, Samson prayed to God one final time. He had lost everything—his strength, his freedom, his sight—but he had not lost his faith. Samson cried out to God with a heart full of humility and repentance. "O Lord God," he prayed, "remember me, I pray thee. Strengthen me, I pray thee, only this once, O God, that I may be avenged of the Philistines for my two eyes."

God heard Samson's prayer. The strength that had once flowed through Samson's body began to return. His muscles tightened, and the power of God filled him once again. Samson knew that this would be his last act, but he was ready to give his life to defeat the enemies of Israel.

With his hands on the pillars, Samson pushed with all his might. At first, nothing happened, but then, slowly, the pillars began to crack. The ground beneath him trembled as the stone columns started to shift. The people in the temple stopped their laughter and looked around in confusion. The laughter turned to fear as the realization dawned that something terrible was happening.

With one final push, Samson brought the pillars crashing down. The entire temple began to collapse, the roof caving in as the walls crumbled around him. Thousands of Philistines were caught in the destruction, including the leaders and lords who had gathered for the feast. The temple of Dagon, the place where Samson had been mocked and humiliated, was now reduced to rubble.

Samson gave his life that day, but in doing so, he defeated more Philistines in his death than he had during his entire life. His final act of courage and strength showed that even in his weakest moment, God was still with him. The Philistines had thought they had won, but in the end, God had used Samson to deliver Israel from their enemies.

After the temple collapsed, Samson's family came to find his body. They took him back to his homeland and buried him in the tomb of his father, Manoah. Though Samson's life had been filled with challenges and mistakes, he had fulfilled his purpose as Israel's champion.

The people of Israel remembered Samson for his great strength, but also for his faith in God. Even in his darkest days, Samson had turned back to the One True God, and God had answered his prayers. Samson's story was a reminder to all of Israel that no matter how far they might fall, God's strength was always there to lift them up.

9

A Prayer for Strength: Samson's Last Hope

Samson had been Israel's mighty warrior for years, but now he found himself in the darkest days of his life. Once the strongest man in all the land, he was now weak, blind, and held captive by the very enemies he had fought against his whole life. The Philistines, who had feared him for so long, now paraded him through the streets in chains. They believed they had finally defeated Samson, and they were determined to make a spectacle of his downfall.

While Samson had lost his physical strength, something else was happening deep inside him. As he toiled in the prison, grinding grain for his enemies, his heart began to change. Samson started to understand that his true strength had never come from his hair alone. It had always come from God, and when Samson turned away from God, he lost not only his strength but also his way.

Samson's hair began to grow again, slowly but surely. It was a reminder that God had not forgotten him, even in his lowest state. As the days passed, Samson's faith began to return. He prayed to God in the quiet moments of his imprisonment, asking for forgiveness and for the strength to fulfill his purpose.

Meanwhile, the Philistines continued to celebrate their victory over Samson. They praised their false god, Dagon, believing that he had delivered Samson into their hands. But the Philistines didn't know the full story. They didn't realize that Samson's true strength came from the One True God, and that

Samson's journey was not yet over.

The Philistine leaders decided to hold a massive feast in the temple of Dagon. They invited thousands of people to gather for the celebration, including all the lords and rulers of the Philistines. The temple was filled with excitement, laughter, and praise for their god. As part of the festivities, the Philistines wanted to bring out Samson so they could mock him in front of the crowd.

Samson, who had once struck fear into their hearts, was now led into the temple by a young servant. The once mighty warrior stumbled blindly, his hands bound in chains. The Philistines laughed and jeered at him, taunting him as they paraded him in front of the crowd. But Samson didn't respond to their insults. Instead, he quietly asked the servant who was leading him, "Let me feel the pillars that support the temple, so I can lean against them."

The servant, thinking nothing of the request, guided Samson to the two central pillars that held up the temple. Samson placed his hands on the pillars, feeling their weight and strength. The crowd continued to mock him, unaware that something incredible was about to happen.

In that moment, Samson prayed to God one final time. His voice was filled with humility and desperation, for he knew this would be his last chance to fulfill the purpose God had given him. "O Lord God," Samson prayed, "remember me, I pray thee, and strengthen me, I pray thee, only this once, O God, that I may be avenged of the Philistines for my two eyes."

Samson knew that he had made many mistakes in his life. He had let his pride and emotions lead him away from God's plan. But in this moment, Samson was not asking for strength to prove himself or to seek personal glory. He was asking for strength to fulfill God's will and to bring justice to the enemies of Israel.

As Samson prayed, the strength he had once known began to return. His muscles tightened, and the power of God filled him once again. Samson gripped the pillars with all his might, feeling the energy surge through his body. This was the strength that had allowed him to defeat lions, tear down city gates, and strike down thousands of Philistines. And now, it was returning to him for one final act.

With all his strength, Samson pushed against the pillars. At first, nothing happened, but Samson did not give up. He pushed harder, and soon, the pillars began to crack. The ground beneath him trembled as the great stone columns shifted. The people in the temple began to notice, but by then, it was too late.

With one final, mighty push, the pillars collapsed, and the entire temple came crashing down. The roof caved in, and the walls crumbled, burying everyone inside, including the Philistine rulers who had gathered for the feast. The Philistines, who had once celebrated their victory over Samson, were now caught in the destruction.

Samson gave his life in that moment, but in doing so, he defeated more Philistines than he had in all his previous battles combined. His final act of strength was not just a victory for Israel, but a reminder that the power of God could never be defeated, even by the strongest enemies.

As the temple lay in ruins, Samson's family came to retrieve his body. They took him back to his homeland and buried him in the tomb of his father, Manoah. Though Samson's life had been filled with mistakes and struggles, he had fulfilled the purpose God had given him. He had been chosen from birth to deliver Israel from the Philistines, and in his final moments, he had done just that.

The people of Israel remembered Samson not only for his great strength, but also for his faith in God. Though he had fallen many times, he had never been abandoned by the One True God. And in the end, Samson's greatest strength was not in his muscles, but in his willingness to trust God, even in his darkest hour.

Samson's story serves as a reminder to all who hear it that true strength comes not from our own abilities, but from our faith in God. No matter how far we fall, God's power is always there to lift us up, just as it was for Samson. And even in our weakest moments, we can find the strength to fulfill God's purpose for our lives.

10

The Final Victory: Samson's Greatest Sacrifice

Samson's life had been filled with extraordinary moments of strength and victory. He had been chosen from birth, a Nazirite dedicated to God, and endowed with a strength unlike any other. For years, he had fought the enemies of Israel, defeating the Philistines time and time again. But despite his great strength, Samson's heart had often led him astray. His decisions had not always been wise, and he had allowed his pride and emotions to guide him into danger.

But in the end, Samson's greatest act was not in the battles he fought with his hands, but in the sacrifice he made to fulfill God's purpose. Samson's story did not end in defeat, but in a final, triumphant victory over the Philistines, a victory that would be remembered by Israel for generations to come.

After his betrayal by Delilah and the loss of his strength, Samson found himself in the darkest days of his life. Blinded and imprisoned by the Philistines, Samson had every reason to believe that his story was over. He had been captured by the very enemies he had spent his life fighting, and it seemed that all hope was lost. But even in his weakest moment, God had not forgotten him.

As Samson's hair began to grow again, so did his faith. Though he was blind, Samson's spiritual sight was being restored. He began to understand that his strength had never truly come from his hair, but from his relationship with the One True God. Samson's heart turned back to God, and he began to pray again, seeking forgiveness and the strength to fulfill the mission he had been given.

The Philistines, however, believed that Samson's defeat was complete. They did not fear him anymore, and they celebrated their victory with great pride. They praised their false god, Dagon, for delivering Samson into their hands, and they planned a grand feast in his honor. Thousands of Philistines gathered in the temple of Dagon, including all the rulers and lords of the Philistine people. They wanted to show off their triumph over Israel's greatest warrior.

As part of their celebration, they brought Samson out of the prison to make a mockery of him. They led him, blind and chained, into the temple, laughing at how far the mighty had fallen. The once powerful Samson, who had struck down thousands of their soldiers, now stumbled helplessly before them. They believed that his strength was gone forever, and they rejoiced in their supposed victory.

But Samson had one last request. As the young servant guided him through the temple, Samson asked quietly, "Let me feel the pillars that support the temple, so I can lean against them." The servant, thinking nothing of it, led Samson to the two central pillars that held up the entire structure.

As Samson stood between the pillars, he prayed to God one final time. His heart was filled with humility and repentance, and he knew that this was his last chance to fulfill the purpose for which he had been born. "O Lord God," Samson prayed, "remember me, I pray thee. Strengthen me, I pray thee, only this once, O God, that I may be avenged of the Philistines for my two eyes."

Samson wasn't asking for strength for his own glory. He wasn't seeking revenge for personal reasons. He was asking God to use him one more time to defeat the enemies of Israel, the enemies of God's people. He was ready to give his life if that was what it would take to fulfill God's will.

God heard Samson's prayer. The strength that had once flowed through Samson's body returned, filling him with the power he had known before. With his hands resting on the pillars, Samson could feel the energy surging through him, the strength that came from God alone. He knew what he had to do.

With all his might, Samson pushed against the pillars. The stones began to shift, and the ground trembled beneath him. The crowd in the temple, which had been laughing and jeering at him, suddenly grew silent as they realized something was happening. Fear spread through the Philistines as the great pillars cracked and crumbled.

Samson gave one final, powerful push, and the pillars collapsed. The entire temple began to cave in, the roof falling in on the thousands of Philistines gathered inside. The great lords and rulers who had come to celebrate their victory over Samson were now caught in the destruction. The temple of Dagon, the false god they had worshiped, was reduced to rubble.

Samson gave his life in that moment, but in doing so, he defeated more Philistines in his death than he had in all his battles combined. His final act of strength was not just a physical victory, but a spiritual one. It was a reminder that the power of the One True God could never be defeated, even by the strongest enemies.

After the temple had fallen, Samson's family came to retrieve his body. They took him back to his homeland and buried him in the tomb of his father, Manoah. Though Samson's life had been filled with mistakes and challenges, he had fulfilled the purpose for which he had been born. He had been chosen by God to deliver Israel from the Philistines, and in the end, he had done just that.

The people of Israel remembered Samson not only for his incredible strength, but also for his faith. Though he had fallen many times, God had never abandoned him. And in his final moments, Samson had turned back to God and completed the mission he had been given.

Samson's story is one of strength, faith, and redemption. It teaches us that no matter how far we may fall, God's grace is always there to lift us up. Samson's greatest victory wasn't in the battles he fought, but in his willingness to trust God, even when all seemed lost.

And so, Samson's legacy lived on, a reminder to all of Israel that true strength comes not from ourselves, but from the One True God who gives us the power to fulfill His purpose.

11

Conclusion

Samson's life was filled with moments of incredible strength and great challenges. From the very beginning, he was chosen by the One True God to deliver Israel from the hands of the Philistines. His strength was unlike any other, but it was not just his muscles that made him powerful—it was his faith in God. Throughout his life, Samson faced many battles, both with his enemies and within his own heart. He made mistakes, acted out of pride, and suffered greatly for his choices.

But in the end, Samson's story is one of redemption. Even when he lost everything—his strength, his freedom, and his sight—God did not abandon him. Samson's final act of sacrifice, in which he gave his life to defeat the Philistines, showed that true strength comes from trusting in God's plan.

Samson's life teaches us that no matter how far we fall, God is always ready to give us the strength we need to fulfill our purpose. His story reminds us that with faith, even the greatest challenges can be overcome, and that God's power is always greater than our own. Samson will forever be remembered as Israel's mighty champion, a hero of faith and strength.

Epilogue

Samson's journey is one of great victories and deep trials, a story that reveals the incredible power of God working through those He chooses. Though Samson's life was filled with challenges—some caused by his own choices—he remained a symbol of the strength that comes from trusting in God. Even in his darkest moments, when all seemed lost, Samson turned back to the One True God, and in doing so, fulfilled his destiny.

His final act of courage and sacrifice was not only a victory over his enemies but a reminder to all of Israel that God's power is always present, even when we falter. Samson's life teaches us that while we may stumble, we are never too far from God's grace. True strength does not come from our own abilities but from our faith in Him.

Samson's story will live on as a testament to God's unwavering love and His willingness to use even the most flawed among us for His purpose. May his life remind us that no matter what battles we face, physical or spiritual, God is always with us, giving us the strength to rise again.

Afterword

The story of Samson is a powerful reminder of the potential we all have when we place our trust in God. Samson was a man blessed with extraordinary strength, but his greatest battles were not with the Philistines—they were with his own heart. His journey was one of incredible highs and painful lows, yet through it all, God's hand remained upon him.

Samson's life teaches us that true strength is not found in physical might alone, but in our willingness to follow God's plan, even when we make mistakes. His failures are reminders that we all stumble at times, but God is always there, ready to give us another chance. It was in his final moments, when Samson turned back to God, that he truly fulfilled his purpose.

This afterword is a reflection on the lessons of Samson's life—lessons of faith, redemption, and the enduring grace of God. His story encourages us to persevere, knowing that even in our weakest moments, God's strength is enough. As we go forward, may we remember that like Samson, we, too, are called to trust in God's plan and rely on His strength to overcome every challenge we face.

About the Author

Michael Southern Sr - Author and Storyteller

I'm Michael Southern Sr, a passionate author and storyteller dedicated to creating engaging and faith-based children's books. With a deep love for storytelling and a commitment to inspiring young minds, my work brings biblical stories to life with vibrant illustrations and relatable narratives. As a parent, I understand the importance of nurturing values like faith, courage, and kindness in our children. That's why each of my books is crafted to spark imagination, encourage curiosity, and provide meaningful lessons that children and families can cherish together.

Through WhimsicalWonders my goal is to share stories that not only entertain but also leave lasting impact. believe in the power of stories to e shape young minds, and I am honored to be Part of that journey. Whether you reading to your child at bedtime or looking for faith-based stories to inspire and teach, hope my books bring joy and wonder into your home.

Also by Michael Southern Sr.

I create engaging and faith-inspired children's books that combine story-telling with valuable life lessons. My work focuses on bringing biblical tales to life in a way that sparks imagination, encourages curiosity, and nurtures young minds. Through vibrant illustrations and relatable narratives, I aim to provide joyful and meaningful reading experiences for children and families

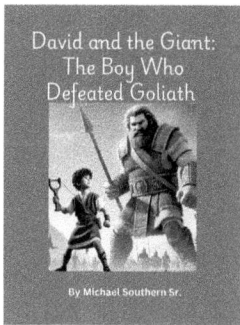

David and the Giant: The Boy Who Defeated Goliath

https://whimsicalwonders54.etsy.com/listing/1787291813/david-and-the-giant-the-boy-who-defeated

When the mighty Goliath threatens Israel, no one dares to face him—except David, a young shepherd boy with unwavering faith. Armed with only a slingshot and five smooth stones, David steps onto the battlefield to face the giant in a battle that will decide the fate of his people. This inspiring retelling of the classic Bible story shows children that with faith in God, even the smallest person can overcome the greatest challenges.

9 798330 583782